Dance and perform with these ballerinas!

# Twirling Ballerinas

It's the day of the big ballet recital! The ballerinas rehearse all of their dance routines. Decorate this picture with the stickers from your sticker sheet.

What musical instrument do you see?

How many bags do you see?

Reward Sticker

# Dressing Room

After their ballet class, the girls get changed into their coats and boots. Use the stickers from your sticker sheet to decorate this picture.

How many scarves can you spot?

What is the bunny holding?

Reward Sticker

# Ballet Costumes

In the dressing room, the ballerinas try on lots of costumes and accessories. Take the stickers from your sticker sheet and decorate this picture.

What is the cat wearing on her face?

How many crowns do you see?

Reward Sticker

# Cinderella

The ballerinas love to dance and twirl in their performance of Cinderella. Decorate this picture with the stickers from your sticker sheet.

How many pumpkins are there?

Use these stickers to complete Twirling Ballerinas!

Use these stickers to complete Dressing Room!

Use these stickers to complete Snow White!

Use these stickers to complete Swan Lake!

**Use these stickers to complete Sleeping Beauty!**

**Reward Stickers**

**Use these stickers to decorate the pages!**

Use these stickers to complete Ballet Costumes!

Use these stickers to complete Cinderella!

What is on the cushion?

Reward Sticker

# Snow White

The ballerinas are having lots of fun performing Snow White. Make this picture look beautiful with your stickers.

## What is the ballerina eating?

How many red apples are there?

Reward Sticker

# Swan Lake

In the Swan Lake ballet, the ballerinas dance in their pretty, feathery tutus. Take the stickers from your sticker sheet and decorate this picture.

How many butterflies can you spot?

What type of animal is dancing?

Reward Sticker

# Sleeping Beauty

The audience adores the performance of Sleeping Beauty.
Everyone claps and cheers for the ballerinas.
Decorate this scene with the stickers.

What type of animal is napping?

How many red flowers are there?

Reward Sticker

# Ballerina Fun

The ballerinas had an amazing time performing in their ballet recital. Use your best crayons, markers, or colored pencils to decorate the ballerinas any way you like!

It's time for some magical fun with these fairies!

# Rainbow Meadow

In Rainbow Meadow, the fairies fly around and play with their animal friends. Use the stickers from your very own sticker sheet to decorate this picture.

**How many birds can you spot?**

What is the little mouse wearing?

Reward Sticker

# Fabulous Flowers

In the flower fields, the fairies cast spells to make the sunflowers grow really tall. Decorate this picture with the stickers from your sticker sheet.

**What picture is on the watering can?**

How many fairies have wands?

Reward Sticker

## Splashy Spells

It's a bright, sunny day, so the fairies cool down in the pond. They love splashing and swimming around. Use your fairy stickers to decorate this lovely picture.

**What animals are on the lily pads?**

How many flowers can you count?

Reward Sticker

# The Wishing Well

The fairies are having fun granting all the animals' wishes by the wishing well. Decorate this picture with your stickers.

**What is the hedgehog wearing?**

Use these stickers to complete Rainbow Meadow!

Use these stickers to complete Fabulous Flowers!

Use these stickers to complete Fairy Forest Party!

Use these stickers to complete Winter Wonderland!

**Use these stickers to complete Goodnight Fairies!**

**Reward Stickers**

**Use these stickers to decorate the pages!**

Use these stickers to complete Splashy Spells!

Use these stickers to complete The Wishing Well!

How many fairies are holding buckets?

Reward Sticker

# Fairy Forest Party

In the enchanted forest, the fairies have a fun party with their animal friends. Make this picture look magical with the stickers from your sticker sheet.

How many mushrooms are there?

**What is on the picnic blanket?**

Reward Sticker

# Winter Wonderland

It's snowing! The fairies love to throw snowballs and skate on the ice. Decorate this winter wonderland with the stickers from your sticker sheet.

**What is the reindeer wearing?**

How many snowballs are there?

Reward Sticker

# Goodnight Fairies

When the sun goes down and the stars come out, the fairies tuck their animal friends into bed. Make this bedtime picture look beautiful with your stickers.

**What is the moon wearing?**

How many fireflies can you count?

Reward Sticker

# Fairy Fun

The fairies had such a fun day playing in Fairy Land. Use your best crayons, markers, or colored pencils to decorate these fairies any way you like!

It's time to have some fun
with your best friend!

# Playtime Friends

Friends love to play together and share their favorite toys. Use the stickers from your sticker sheet to decorate this bedroom picture.

Which animal is in its cage?

How many crayons are there?

Reward Sticker

# Busy Bakers

It's time to bake some delicious cakes in the kitchen, but try not to make a big mess! Decorate this picture with lots of stickers.

How many pancakes are there?

What is the cat carrying?

Reward Sticker

# Splish Splash Swimmers

There's nothing like splashing and diving in the swimming pool! Decorate the picture with the stickers from your sticker sheet.

How many balls do you see?

Which animal is wearing goggles?

Reward Sticker

# Pretty Play Park

What's your favorite thing to do on the playground? Decorate the picture with lots of stickers from your sticker sheet.

**Which animal is on the swings?**

Use these stickers to complete Playtime Friends!

Use these stickers to complete Busy Bakers!

Use these stickers to complete Cool Carnival!

Use these stickers to complete Super Sweet Store!

# Use these stickers to complete Sleepover Time!

## Reward Stickers

Use these stickers to decorate the pages!

# Use these stickers to complete Splish Splash Swimmers!

# Use these stickers to complete Pretty Play Park!

How many butterflies can you see?

Reward Sticker

# Cool Carnival

The carnival is in town! Decorate the picture with stickers from your sticker sheet.

**What does the bunny have in its mouth?**

How many balloons are there?

Reward Sticker

# Super Sweet Store

The candy store is filled with all kinds of yummy candy and chocolate! Decorate this picture with stickers.

How many lollipops do you see?

Which animal is climbing on the table?

Reward Sticker

# Sleepover Time

Make this the best sleepover ever! Decorate the picture with lots of stickers from your very own sticker sheet.

**How many bowls of candy are there?**

Which animal is sleeping on the bed?

Reward Sticker

# Friends Fun

The best friends had a great sleepover.
They have never had so much fun! Use your favorite
crayons, markers, and colored pencils to decorate
the girls any way you like!

Get ready to go to the royal ball with these princesses!

# Pretty Palace

The princesses arrive at the palace for the royal party. They can't wait to see each other! Decorate this picture with lots of stickers.

**What is the bird holding in her beak?**

How many daisies are on the ground?

Reward Sticker

# Princess Picnic

The princesses have a lovely picnic in the palace gardens. Decorate this picture with the stickers from your sticker sheet.

**What are the princesses eating?**

How many unicorns can you spot?

Reward Sticker

# Baking Fun

The princesses have lots of fun baking cakes in the palace kitchen. Use the stickers from your sticker sheet to decorate this picture.

How many cookies can you count?

What is the baker holding?

Reward Sticker

# Royal Dance Room

The princesses are dressed up and dancing to the piano music. Make this picture look fabulous with the stickers from your sticker sheet.

**What shape is on the purple bag?**

Use these stickers to complete Pretty Palace!

Use these stickers to complete Princess Picnic!

Use these stickers to complete Dress Shopping!

Use these stickers to complete Gorgeous Gowns!

**Use these stickers to complete Dazzling Princesses!**

**Reward Stickers**

**Use these stickers to decorate the pages!**

Use these stickers to complete Baking Fun!

Use these stickers to complete Royal Dance Room!

How many mice are there?

Reward Sticker

# Dress Shopping

At the shopping mall, the princesses buy their dresses for the royal party. Find the stickers on your sticker sheet and decorate this picture with them.

What is the cat wearing?

What is the puppy carrying?

Reward Sticker

# Gorgeous Gowns

In the dressing room, the princesses get dressed for the royal party. Decorate this picture with the stickers from your sticker sheet.

How many dresses are hanging on the rack?

Where are the mice playing?

Reward Sticker

# Dazzling Princesses

The princesses have an amazing time dancing at the royal party. Use the stickers from your sticker sheet to decorate this picture.

**What type of juice is in the jug?**

How many balloons can you count?

Reward Sticker

# Princess Fun

The princesses had a wonderful time at the royal party!
Use your favorite crayons, markers, or colored pencils
to decorate these princesses any way you like!